The Rockwool Foundation Research Unit

Study Paper No. 75

Competition or cooperation?

A longitudinal case study of NPM reforms' influence on strategic management in upper secondary schools

*Jesper Rosenberg Hansen and
Christian Bøtcher Jacobsen*

University Press of Southern Denmark

Odense 2014

Competition or cooperation?

A longitudinal case study of NPM reforms' influence on strategic management in upper secondary schools

Study Paper No. 75

Published by:
© The Rockwool Foundation Research Unit

Address:
The Rockwool Foundation Research Unit
Soelvgade 10, 2.tv.
DK-1307 Copenhagen K

Telephone	+45 33 34 48 00
E-mail	forskningsenheden@rff.dk
web site:	www.en.rff.dk

ISBN 978-87-93119-17-8
ISSN 0908-3979

August 2014

Competition or cooperation? A longitudinal case study of NPM reforms' influence on strategic management in upper secondary schools

Jesper Rosenberg Hansen

Christian Bøtcher Jacobsen

ABSTRACT

NPM reforms are often argued to promote efficiency, because they enhance strategic and competitive behaviour among public organisations. Oppositely, critics argue that strategic behaviour can be problematic for public organizations, because cooperation and collaboration is needed to increase the general public value rather than just maximizing organizational profit. In this paper, we study how an NPM reform (introducing self-government for upper secondary schools coupled with quasi-markets with activity based funding) in the Danish secondary school sector changes strategic management both in regard to strategic orientation and strategic processes. We apply a panel case study design over a 10 year period - 3 rounds of interviews with five school principals before, during, and after reform (2002/3, 2009, and 2012) combined with secondary data (documents and register data). The results show a clear build-up in strategic management over the period of study though the strategic process is not entirely formalized. However, though competition is more prevalent than before the reform, strong institutions maintain a substantial level of collaboration between schools. Furthermore, there are substantial variations in the schools' strategic management. The results show that NPM reforms will most likely force public organisations to adapt their strategic management to some extent, but that the organisations' environment in the form collective and cooperative institutions and individual opportunities and threats can dampen the effects substantially, at least in the shorter run.

Keywords: strategic management, competition, cooperation, New Public Management

INTRODUCTION

In recent decades, a number of vast reforms have changed the functioning of many public service areas from traditional hierarchical governance to market-inspired coordination (Pollitt & Bouckaert 2011). These reforms have been expected to have important consequences for the strategic management within the individual organizations and for the interaction between organizations (Christensen & Pallesen 2001). Thus, organizations have been expected to be in a more competitive stance towards one another, which is why they have been believed to be more oriented towards their strategic positions and possibilities (Hansen & Ferlie 2013). In general strategic management can be important in public sector organizations, because it can improve a number of desired organizational outcomes (Moore 1995; Poister et al. 2010). Strategic management has also mostly been shown to have a positive effect on performance though there is need for more and especially new type of research (Boyne & Walker 2010). There is little knowledge on whether and how NPM reforms induce public organizations to become more strategically oriented (Hansen & Ferlie 2013). And we do not know whether NPM reforms affect public organization to become more private-like (Hood 1991, Beckett 2000) and influence public organizations' strategic management and action. This also goes in relation to whether they become more competitive and less cooperative in relation to other public organizations. The critics argue that NPM reforms make public organizations focused only on competition and thereby lack focus on the broader collaboration in regard to achieving public value, which is argued to be the key focus of public organizations (Christensen & Lægreid 2007). This relates to the issue about single purpose public organizations, which aim for simple goals instead of focusing on the overall complex goals, which are of societal value (Rainey 2009; Gregory 2006; Pollitt 2003). Such one-sided focus on competition is also argued to challenge the normative foundations of public sector organizations (Peters & Pierre 1998; Olsen 2006), and the general focus on market orientation are by some argued to have gone too far in public sector (Walker,

Boyne, Brewer & Avellaneda 2011). Thus, market failures may harm the combined welfare produced, when numerous players fail to handle problems related to collective action problems (Olson, 1971; Christensen & Lægreid 2007). Finally, there are numerous examples on the unintended effects of competitive oriented NPM reforms (Andersen & Serritzlew 2007, Le Grand 2010, Soss, Fording & Schram 2011). Summing up, there are numerous reasons why we need a deeper understanding of how public organizations respond to NPM reforms.

In this paper, we look into the line of research, which argues that organizations will take a more strategic stance, when they have high administrative autonomy, when their budgets are based on performance, and when they face market-like structures (Hansen & Ferlie 2013) such as quasi-markets (Ferlie 1992). In recent years a number of NPM-inspired reforms throughout public sectors in Western countries have to varying degrees introduced exactly these three aspects. We expect that in areas where such reforms are introduced, managers become more strategically oriented (Hansen & Ferlie 2013). However, we know very little about how this transition to strategic management plays out, and whether competition will be the key aspect or the public organizations will keep cooperating.

Traditionally, public organizations have functioned in hierarchical settings, and in multi-agency settings horizontal coordination (Scharpf, 1994) is often characterized by cooperation (Christensen & Lægreid 2007). Thus, in many areas formal networks have institutionalized cooperative norms, and allowed organizations to coordinate their actions according to their collective interest. In reformed settings these institutions may persist and thereby maintain cooperation, but they are also challenged, because the reforms favour competition over cooperation (Le Grand 2009). When organizations are faced with "profit" motives, they are also tempted to break the collective norms, because the pay-off is now much more evident than in the hierarchical setting. Organizations in a more competitive context have much to gain from strategic management, whereas a cooperative environment makes strategic management less needed. Thus, a competitive environment is expected to force organizations to think and act more strategically in regard to the organization's own interests than organizations in a cooperative environment. Therefore, the cooperative institutions are under pressure. The main aim of this paper is to understand how an NPM reform changes public organizations' strategic decision-making and behaviour, since we have very little knowledge about organizational strategic adaptation processes (Hansen 2011). Thus, the paper addresses the following research questions: *Has the structural reform among secondary schools in Denmark introduced more strategic management and behaviour, and has this increased the competition and reduced cooperation between the schools?*

The research design is a ten year longitudinal case study of five Danish upper secondary schools, which due to the Danish Structural Reform in 2007 (The Danish Ministry of the Interior and Health 2004) experienced dramatic changes in their context (Principals' Association 2011). The schools obtained more autonomy and are now self-governing with their own supervisory boards, and their financing depends to a large extent on the number of enrolled students and students passing exams (The Danish Ministry of the Interior and Health 2004). We investigate whether these changes in conditions result in more formalized strategies, especially more externally focused competitive strategies, and how different schools apply strategic management due to specific factors such as school size, geographical placement and specialization. The study applies a unique panel structure based on qualitative interviews with key people at five different Danish secondary schools combined with background interviews with bureaucrats and representatives from interest organizations as well register data. The interviews at the five schools were conducted in three rounds in 2003, 2008 and 2012. The principals were interviewed about their understanding of strategic leadership/management, how they work with strategy, what their most important strategic issues are including their relationship to other schools. We therefore have a unique opportunity to study how strategy has developed from before the reform was introduced to immediately after implementation and up to now, where the reform is well in place. We can therefore both look at how the school talk about strategy and how they act, and whether they compete or cooperate.

In the theory section below, we focus on strategic management in public organizations and how NPM reforms can be expected to influence both the strategic orientation and the strategic processes in processes in regard to both the internal and external aspects. Furthermore, we argue that competition is often a key aspect in NPM reforms, and that this may run counter with traditional collaboration between public organizations. In the method section we look at the empirical setting of Danish secondary schools, the design of the case study and data analysis strategy. In the analysis section we show that the schools are becoming more strategic – yet not necessarily in a formalized way, and that schools are also beginning to focus on competition at the expense of collaboration. We also show that the schools have in different ways increased focus on the school profile and also look for new ways through mergers and larger corporative arrangements. The paper ends with a discussion of the results and suggestions for future research on the embedded conflicts in many public sector reforms between competition and collaboration.

STRATEGIC MANAGEMENT AND STRATEGIC BEHAVIOUR IN THE PUBLIC SECTOR

Strategic management is often defined as determination of the long-term goal and objectives of the organizations and adopting the action and resource allocation to these goals (Chandler 1962) and also about matching the organization with its environment (Hofer & Schendel 1978). Moreover, in the generic strategic management literature the main focus is on insuring a sustainable competitive advantage compared to other organizations. However, in the public administration literature it is often argued that public and private organizations are distinct in regard to strategic management (Nutt & Backoff 1993; Moore 2000; Ring & Perry 1985). Several authors have pointed to the fact that public organizations are not established for the purpose of profit creation, as private organizations are, but instead to create public value (Moore 1995). Public organizations thereby focus on achieving a social mission for the stakeholders (Moore 2000). They have to satisfy an overall mandate which often is complex and dependent on other public entities and they also have multiple stakeholders to consider (Bryson 2004). Though strategic management in public organizations can have different orientations from more or less external or internal orientation (Johanson 2009), strategic management in public organizations have therefore traditionally not focused on competition like in private organizations. Instead the main focus has been collaboration and cooperation between public organizations (McGuire 2006; Nutt and Backoff 1993; Koontz & Thomas, 2006).

In opposition to the view just sketched above, New Public Management reforms are often argued to make strategic management more important in public organizations (Bryson, Berry & Yang 2010, Hansen & Ferlie 2013), because increased environmental pressure forces public organizations to become more attentive towards their long run scope and direction (Ferlie 2003). Thus, NPM regimes are expected to make public organizations more focused on aspects such as their competitive stance, maintaining an adequate demand for services, and lowering the income/cost ratio. When market-inspired structures such as activity based budgeting and self-governing are introduced, public organizations increasingly use strategic tools such as SWOT analysis, environment analysis, and analyses of position and competitors (Hansen 2011). However, the structural changes may affect organizations very differently depending on environmental variations (Hansen 2011). If organizations are in fact local monopolies, they may be much less inclined to adapt to the structural pressure (Andersen & Serritzlew 2007). Furthermore, collaborative arrangements from before the reform may lead to some level of path dependency (Pierson 2000), because institutionalized norms and arrangements make it costly or unrealistic to deviate from earlier behavioural patterns. We therefore address the need for more in-depth studies of how public organizations apply strategic management in the wake of reforms (Ferlie 2003). This study investigates how public organizations apply strategic management and especially whether and how organizations in various environmental settings adapt their use of strategy, when the settings are changed to resemble those of the private sector. These NPM reforms could be expected to influence public organizations' strategic orientation and strategic processes. Hence, the reform may have both internal effects, because the public organizations will be forced to change their strategic decision-making, and also external effects, because the public organizations will change the way they interact with their environment and perhaps even shift to a more competitive stance.

NPM reforms cover a wide array of efforts, but to understand adaptation of strategic action more fully, it is important to understand the exact type of change implied by the reform. In this paper, the reform under study involves a sector-wide introduction of quasi-markets (Le Grand 1991), which affects rather similar public organizations (upper secondary schools). The concept of quasi-markets in general build on the notion that the organizations need to compete for their funding with other providers, which could be both public organizations, non-profit organizations and/or private companies (Ferlie 1992). These quasi-markets are today found in most New Public Management influenced countries as this introduction of competition is a key part of NPM (Ferlie 2003). An abundant literature on quasi-market in both health care (Ferlie 1992, Le Grand, 1991) and schools (Whitty 1997, Bradley, Crouchley, Millington & Taylor 2000, Glennerster 1991) witnesses the wide application of quasi-markets and look into the both intended and unintended consequences of marketization. These studies also show that quasi markets come in several different forms, and that these arrangements span from contracting to actual quasi market (Le Grand 1991; Ferlie 1992). We focus on an ambitious reform, which grants consumers/citizens some extent of choice between service providers, but which is on the other hand a rather simple case with fixed prices (set by the central Danish government and passed in Parliament). This quasi-market reform involves only public organizations, which are relatively free to cooperate, but for analytical purposes we see that as an advantage, because it presents a relatively hard case in relation to strategic management. The organizations can either focus very narrowly on their own organizational interests, or they can maintain cooperation between schools for their joint interest. Another option is to cooperate with organizations, which were not collaborates prior to the reform in order to be in a better competition with former collaborators. This joint competition and cooperation situation is in the private management literature termed *co-opetition* (Bengtsson & Kock 2000; Gnyawali, He & Radhavan 2006, Walley 2007), and it has also been studied in the public sector (Hooks & Palakshappa 2009) including schools (Adnette & Davies 2003). We are therefore interested in how public organizations think and act strategically, when they operate in quasi-markets, and especially how they think and act in regard to competition and cooperation with other public organizations.

However, while there have been studies on the effects of strategic management using rather simple measures of strategy types, (e.g. there is a huge literature on the impact of Miles and Snow prospector, defenders and reactors on performance e.g. Andrews, Boyne, Law & Walker 2009, Meier, O'Toole, Boyne & Walker 2007) there is generally a lack of studies of how public organization behave in practice (Bryson et. al 2010). There are few comprehensive case studies of strategic management in regard to the strategic management and action (for an exception see Llewellyn & Tappin 2003) and to our knowledge there are no existing studies have applied longitudinal case studies of strategic management changes over a reform period.

Typically, the strategic decision-making processes of public organizations are not oriented towards competitive environments, and for all we know they are instead both more bureaucratic and directed at stakeholder satisfaction rather than shareholders (Boyne 2002). Furthermore, public managers are 'less likely to support budget decisions backed by analysis and more likely to support those that are derived from bargaining with agency people' (Nutt 2006). Thus, managers in hierarchically governed public organizations are more inclined to maintain internal organizational aspects, because they see bargaining with peers and subordinates as sanctifying the effort, and the strategic decision making process resembles political processes. Oppositely, private sector managers place a greater emphasis on analysis, and the unilateral top managerial responsibility over strategic decisions. This latter criteria is linked to keeping levels of conflict as low as possible in the attempt to make quick and clear decisions (Amason 1996). The literature on strategic decision making says little about reform processes, but it can be expected that if public organizations are forced to become more strategic in their doings, they are also forced to adapt their internal processes and resemble private organizations to higher degrees. Thus, when public organizations are exposed to more competitive environments, a vital step is the transformation of the strategic decision-making processes.

STUDY DESIGN AND METHODS

The area of study is Danish upper secondary schools which have traditionally functioned in a traditional hierarchical setting under the administrative responsibility of the former counties. Thus, the former setting was a traditional administrative arrangement based on hierarchy and generally characterized by limited influence of New Public Management. However, in 2007 the Danish Structural Reform introduced dramatic changes in these schools' context (The Danish Ministry of the Interior and Health 2004). The schools obtained more autonomy and are now self-governing with their own supervisory boards. They have responsibility for more tasks: e.g. deciding which specialized study areas to supply to the students, and in the long run defining their capacity for students etc. Furthermore, their budgets have changed from fixed to output-purchase budgeting, which means that their budgets depend on the number of students enrolled and students passing exams. Hence, the schools are now in a more competitive situation in relation to recruiting and retaining students. Before the reform, schools were ensured with a number of students, because students were allocated to the different schools by a public committee. Still, at a broader level upper secondary schools remain public organizations because they are publicly owned and funded, and they are still limited by their mandate.

The analysis of the research question is based on a longitudinal case study of five schools within the same geographical region in Denmark. These schools have earlier been under the jurisdiction of the same county, and they have (along with six other schools) worked in close collaboration in relation to particularly the distribution of students. These cases were chosen to keep the overall administrative setting constant and at the same time to ensure variety on a number of dimensions (will be discussed below). The selection of cases within the same administrative setting has both advantages and weaknesses. It is a weakness in relation to external validity, because the administrative environment was characterized by particularly high levels of cooperation before the reform, and this may very well influence the possibilities for strategic management and competitive behaviour. On the other hand, this can also be seen as a conservative test for the effects of NPM reforms. Furthermore, it is an advantage, that the schools were regulated equally before the reform, to ensure a common baseline.

The case selection should also ensure variation in relation to size, specialization, and geographical locations (see Table 1 for an overview). Regarding size we study a large urban school (almost 700 students) in the one end and a small rural school and a small rural school (around 300 students) in the other end. Regarding urbanization we have the large urban school and a preparation course in a larger Danish city, while the other schools are in rural areas nearby (between 20 and 40 kilometres from the larger city). In relation to specialization we see that especially the preparation course is narrowly specialized (they have only the preparation course, which is an abbreviated two-year education with many similarities to the ordinary gymnasium), and another school is partly boarding and international school. Furthermore the minor rural school also tries to find areas of specialization while for the midsized rural school and the large urban school both have broader specialization.

Table 1. Case selection sorted by environment and specialization (selection made in 2003)

		Specialization	
		Little specialization	*High specialization*
Environment	*Urban*	School A: Large urban school	School B: Small school with preparation course
	Rural	School C: Midsized rural school School D: Small rural school	School E: Midsized school with boarding and international schools

DATA AND STRATEGY FOR THE ANALYSIS

We have interviewed the principal at all schools three times - before, during and after reform implementation (2003, 2008, and 2012, see Figure 1 below). We have also interviewed most deputy principals as well as board members, experts, and key people in different organizations and interest groups, e.g. the Ministry of Education, the Principals Association and people from the former counties. The interviews lasted between one and three hours. All interviews were recorded electronically, fully transcribed, and coded with the qualitative analysis software, NVivo.

The strategy for analysing the interviews was divided in two steps. First, to ensure a valid and reliable coding outcome, a predefined list of codes was made on the basis of central concepts related to strategic management (see Appendix A). The coding was open, so we added a few codes during the first round of coding, and statements were coded on several codes when necessary. Second, following the suggestions of Miles and Huberman (1994) we made a data reduction where we discarded all irrelevant information and selected coded interview statements were condensed and systematically summarized into displays. These displays compare the use of strategic management across the three periods and across different types of schools. These displays are presented in the following section. Since the displays presented here are extremely condensed, we have also added some of the most relevant statements in the analysis of the results. Finally, the case study also exploits different sources of written material: e.g. reports, board memos, strategies, and register data, and these are also used throughout the analysis.

Figure 1. Timeline depicting important reform steps and interviews

| | 2005: | 2007: | | 2010: | |
	Reform approved	*Reform commencement*		*Reform fully implemented*	
2003:			**2008:**		**2012:**
Interview 1			Interview 2		Interview 3

Figure 2 shows that all schools have dramatically increased their intake of students throughout the entire period of study. The Danish youth are increasingly seeking towards ordinary upper secondary education (gymnasium) at the expense of vocational training and mercantile educations. Hence, this is a study of reform efforts in good times, and as we will discuss below this may have an impact on both the extent of strategic management and especially on the level of competition between schools.

Figure 2. Student population, 2001-11 (Index, large urban, 2011 =100)

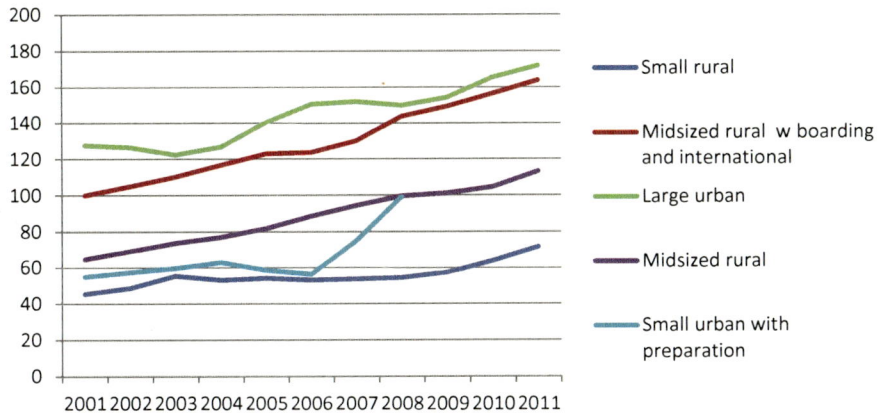

FINDINGS

The analysis of the reform effects is made in relation to both strategic process and strategic orientation where we interested in understanding how NPM may influence these both internally and externally. In the theoretical section we argued that the schools will most likely become more competitively oriented than they were before the NPM reform, and that they will also direct some strategic orientation towards their internal aspects related to efficiency. Furthermore, we argued that the reform will most likely force the schools to pay much more attention to the strategic process and to make it more responsive and management driven. Finally, we look at the variations in strategic management between schools in different geographical locations and with varying degrees of specialization.

Strategic orientation

Prior to the reform, the schools were only strategically oriented to a minimal degree, and the principals were generally not prioritizing strategy much. Instead they emphasized their role as managers of a public service organization, which delivered service alongside similar organizations. One principal says that *That is not a word we use on a daily basis [...] there is not much room for such contemplations.* The lack of strategic management also became clear to another principal, who in retrospect described the attitude towards strategic thinking: *It would be as strange as asking the manager of a main post office what their profile is. He would say that they are just the biggest post office in town, and that if you want to know about the purpose of the post offices, you can ask the central office in Copenhagen* (Small rural, 2008). Hence, when the principals talk about strategy, they are alienated by the concept, they are rather imprecise towards the actual content, and the few formal documents on strategy reveal that the focus is rather unclear and internally oriented. Furthermore, the internal strategic considerations are not on efficiency but rather on effectiveness in the form of quality teaching and stakeholder well-being. The external considerations are mainly on cooperation with the surrounding schools and on maintaining student intake, and these cooperative behaviours are so strong that one principal says that: *A strategy is often made among the principals, though that is not what we call it.* (Urban preparatory, 2003).

When the reform was under implementation in 2008, the schools had been granted much more autonomy, and the activity based funding system had just been introduced, but the principals were not so familiar with the changes. The boards, which had been granted much more formal power and instilled with more competent members, were in place, but the schools had not yet taken over the buildings. Despite the *under construction* atmosphere of the time, the schools had clearly become more strategically oriented, though cooperation was still the order of the day. First of all, schools had been forced to consider their course supply and thereby their profiles towards potential students. In this venture, the schools had also become more aware of the competition with the other schools, though it did not play a prominent role in their strategic management and behaviour. Instead cooperation remained the dominant approach. One principal sums it up this way: *Competition has sharpened and so has the tone. [...] but it springs from the network and the mutual agreements we make on how to act, and this has positive diverted effects on the competition.* (Midsized rural, 2008). In this case positive effects on competition mean dampening and not enhancing, so it also reveals that from a principal's viewpoint, competition is not so attractive. Nonetheless, some schools also took rather drastic measures to adapt to the reform. For the smallest school (urban preparatory) it was economically difficult to continue without subsidies from the county, and it therefore accepted a merger with a larger school, which diminished its status to division. Another school (midsized rural) invited a local mercantile school to share its buildings to keep down costs, but these schools remained organisationally separate. Another small school (small rural) was under significant economic pressure, and the principal therefore considered opportunities of collaboration with schools in neighbouring areas. Generally, the schools had internally become much more aware of their financial situation, and since they were now fully responsible for their own budgets, the newly promoted boards and the principals had generally taken a more long run perspective on the economic developments. Since passing students were equivalent with more money for the schools, they also emphasized student retention much more than earlier.

Table 3. Strategic orientation before, during, and after implementation of reforms.

	Pre-reform (2003)	Reform implementation (2008)	Post reform (2012)
Overall use of strategic management	Weak and informal	Some but informal	Some and formalizing
External orientation			
School cooperation	+	+	(+)
School competition	-	(-)	(+)
Student intake	+	+	+
Growth	-	(+)	(+)
School profile	-	+	+
Internal orientation			
Quality of teaching	+	+	+
Student retention	-	(+)	+
Student well-being	(+)	(+)	+
Teacher well-being	+	+	(+)
Financial situation	-	(+)	+
Efficiency (output/input)	-	(-)	(+)

-: No orientation, (-): weak orientation, (+) some orientation, +: Strong orientation

In 2012, the reform was more or less fully implemented. After a few years of self-government, the schools had become more acquainted with their new rights and duties, and they had taken over their buildings from the state. Cooperation remains to a large extent, and a principal directly ascribes this to the cooperative traditions and the consensus seeking and highly influential principal of the largest urban school: *If we did not have this good cooperation around the distribution of students and the chairman of the distribution council also had that opinion, there would in fact be a problem* (midsized rural, 2012). This quote implies that without the cooperative traditions, competition would be much fiercer, and both this principal and others refer directly to the situation in other geographical areas, where competition is apparently much harsher. The consensus seeking chairman of the distribution council in fact argues that competition has turned up much more in their area: *These rural schools are lurching on one another on what to play and when. […] So yes, the cooperative culture is definitely under pressure now* (large urban school). According to him, the rural schools are facing a lower demand for their services, and they are therefore tempted to compete more for students. Internally, student wellbeing and retention are key aspects, which should probably be seen in relation to the significance for funding. Importantly, the principals report that they teacher well-being.

Overall, the results on strategic orientation show that principals' were initially and before the reform only strategic to a very limit degree, but that this has changed to some extent after the reform. Significant changes took place immediately after the reform, and these changes were somewhat enhanced when the reform was fully implemented. After reform implementation the schools were strategically oriented towards both internal and external aspects, and it is particularly interesting to see how schools are at the same time somewhat competitively oriented and attempting to maintain cooperation between schools. Whether cooperation is maintained for the schools own sake or due to strong institutions will be discussed below.

Strategic processes

Not only the strategic orientation but also the strategic process has changed substantially over the reform period. Before the reform, the sparse strategic decision making was characterised by broad consensus and internal bargaining, meaning that nearly all decisions about strategy were discussed in various school councils with representation by the teachers. In fact the principals more or less agree that though the teachers' council (*pædagogisk råd*) was only advisory, it was not wise for any principal to make decisions without its consent. This is clear among all the principals and stated clearly by one who says that: *We nearly never go against a vote in the teachers' council* (Midsized rural w boarding 2003), and in retrospect another one says that: *In the old world, we could not decide anything, if it had not been debated in the teachers' council for half a year.* (Small rural, 2008). This strategic making process seems to cause a conservative strategic orientation, because the teachers are often focused on maintaining status quo to secure their benefits in the existing system. Oppositely, the weak boards meant next to nothing before the reform, and they did generally not participate actively in the strategic decision-making process: *Formally, of course, the board has competence to decide the budget, but in reality, they have no interest* (Large urban 2003). The principal plays the role of a bargainer, who has to consider his options against the county externally and the teachers internally. The application of strategic tools is very sparse, and the few tools are very ad hoc and indeed informal.

During reform implementation the strategic process changed quite a lot. The teachers' role diminished somewhat, and on one school the principal tells a short story about how he cut off the teachers from influence: *The chairman of the teachers' council sometimes said that we needed to debate that in the teachers' council and that we cannot have that. I said 'Why actually, and where does it say so?'*. (Small rural, 2008). Another principal says that *there is not the same expectation of inclusion of the teachers' council in all affairs* (Large urban 2008). According to the principals the teachers' collective access to strategic decision making has been breached, and instead he and his colleagues aim at including more proactive teachers, who are not necessarily against changes. This more flexible decision making process seems to have been somewhat effective. Another substantial change is the much enhanced role of the board, which has been given considerable formal competencies in relation to both strategies and management. This is also a challenge for some of the principals: *You are more alone in relation to the board than the group of principals was before in relation to the council* (Large urban 2008). Nonetheless, it is clear that both board and managers are adapting to this new situation at this early stage, and that most boards are initially pretty cautious. This cautiousness may also reflect that several board members including the chairman have in this period of establishment been appointed by the principal. Nonetheless, the managers and the boards have gained substantially more influence on strategic decisions, but they must still pay attention to the teachers who are in the end responsible for deciding and not least carrying out strategic decisions. The schools have adapted some strategic tools, and some have made for example SWOT analyses, but mainly the strategic tools remain informal.

After the reforms have been fully implemented, the consensus structure has eroded even more. One school, the largest and most popular one, upholds a structure of wide consensus, but at the other schools, the principals are mainly discussing strategic decisions with teacher representatives. The broader group of teachers is oriented about decisions, and the principals are still to some degree dependent of the teachers' consent, but they seek the commitment of teacher representatives on common decisions. Furthermore, several principals have compensated the teachers by granting them more direct access to non-strategic decisions such as classroom aspects through a number of specialist councils. The board plays an important role in initiation and evaluation of the strategic decisions, but it is only in one school (Midsized rural w boarding), where the board is actually the driving force behind the strategic decision-making. This school has applied a very formalized strategic decision-making process with annually adapted strategic plans, results contracts cascaded down to the middle-managers, and the budget and accounting process not only involves financial aspects but also strategically formulated goals. In the other four schools, the manager has great influence by setting the agenda on the strategic discussions. The boards in these schools do have their own ideas on the strategic decisions, but most of the strategic management seems to be initiated by the principal. The strategic tools used in these schools are less formal than in the midsized school w boarding.

Table 2. Display of strategic decision-making process before, during, and after implementation of reforms.

	Pre-reform	Reform implementation	Post reform
Decision-making	Broad consensus	Managed broad consensus	Managed narrow consensus
Actor roles			
- Principal	Bargainer	Pivotal	Pivotal
- Board	Decoupled	Sparring partner	Co-initiator and sparring partner
- Teachers	Veto player	Representative	Representative
Strategic tools			
- Application	Sparse	Some	Wide
- Formalization	Ad hoc and informal	Mostly ad hoc and few formal tools	Some ad hoc and some formal tools

Note: Content is condensed on the basis of the 15 interviews and shows general trends only.

Summing up on strategic process, it is clear that the process has changed dramatically during the reform period. Before the reform, the teachers were a pivotal actor with veto opportunities towards most central strategic decisions. This has changed substantially with the reform, so that the principal and the board are now in charge of the strategic decision making process. This does not mean that the teachers play no role for strategic decision-making at all, but they are much less dominant than they used to be. Also the strategic tools have become much more widely applied and formal.

Variations in strategic management among schools

Before the reform, the strategic management practices at the five schools under study varied only little. However, the schools are facing rather different strategic weaknesses and opportunities, and given the pressure applied with the NPM reforms, it is relevant to see how the strategic management varies after the reform.

In relation to specialization, it could be expected that more specialized schools need to be more attentive to their strategies in order to meet a more specific demand than the schools with only ordinary education (gymnasium). The ordinary schools face a very stable demand, and the students have much information about the educations they supply. Looking at Table 4, we can get an idea of the significance of specialization by comparison across similar environments. Comparing the urban schools, we see that the specialized school is somewhat more strategically oriented and that the process is more managed than at the ordinary school. The rural schools show a similar picture, though the level of strategic management is generally higher. Thus, the specialized school applies the highest levels of strategic management in relation to both orientation and process. Though this is not evidence that specialization leads to more strategic management, it supports our expectation.

Table 4. Strategic orientation and use of strategic management *after* reform for different types of schools

		Specialization	
		Only ordinary	*Specialized*
Environment	Urban	Large urban: *Orientation:* Weak, internal *Process:* Broad consensus	Urban preparatory: *Orientation:* Modest, internal and some external *Process:* Managed narrow consensus (close coordination with upper tier)
	Rural	Midsized rural and small rural: *Orientation:* Modest, internal and external *Process:* Managed broad consensus	Midsized rural w boarding *Orientation:* Strong, internal and external *Process:* Managed narrow consensus

Next, looking at the environment, we expect that the rural schools are more strategically oriented than the urban schools, because they face a lower demand, since most students are seeking towards the city. If we first compare the ordinary schools, we see that both rural schools are much more strategically oriented and that the process is more managed than at the urban school. According to the manager at the urban school this may have to do with his privileged position with excessive demand, so that he can *afford his neglect of strategic thinking* (Large urban, 2012). Comparing the specialized schools, we also see that the rural school is by far the most strategic one in relation to both orientation and process. The rural school has applied a rather formalized strategic management practice, whereas the urban school is more internally focused.

Summing up, both geographical position in a rural area and a specialized supply is related with stronger strategic management. Now we will discuss this finding and the earlier findings.

CONCLUDING DISCUSSION

The study has shown that NPM reforms can alter the strategic management and behaviour of public secondary schools. Externally, schools become much more oriented towards their 'market position', and they are more competitively oriented in the sense that they are concerned with the distribution of students between schools. Particularly, the smaller schools, which face a lower demand for their services, are concerned with their strategic position, and they have therefore applied more strategic management. Nonetheless, despite this adaptation to a more competitive posture, it is remarkable how much all principals stress the continued importance of collaboration between schools. The school principals are in strong network structures, where rather stable institutions maintain the cooperative behaviour.

Internally, the schools change from broad consensus and bargaining structures to more managed strategic setups, where the focal point for strategic decisions is lifted to the board and management levels. Especially the principals and boards get a stronger role while the teachers get their strategic role reduced significantly. The larger impact of management is one of the clear goals with NPM reforms in general as part of the managerialism (Pollitt 1990) and the urge to let managers manage (Kettl 1997). This study emphasizes that this is often on behalf of other actors, here teachers. This is not necessarily a bad thing for the teachers, since they are provided opportunities to get heard by the principal in more professionally oriented areas, and they are thereby allowed to focus on their teaching. Thus, the deadlock of the old system is somewhat breached.

We see that the introduction of this quasi market does not at once introduce competition, but it is slowly beginning to show its impact. Especially it could be argued that the schools are trying to prepare for the potential increased competition incurred by fewer students (due to diminishing cohorts) by making major changes – we see schools merge, sharing buildings with other schools, and that the schools in general strengthen their profiles. However, the principals in general do not talk about major increases in competition yet. The first two rounds of interviews also revealed that the schools were still governed by the pre-reform structure, where there was much focus on cooperation between the regional government and the schools and also regionally between the schools. A unique regional governance seems to have influenced how the schools compete after the reform - and also how they use strategic management - due to an informal agreement not to compete intensely, and this could be interpreted as a sort of path dependence explanation (Pierson 2000) A rivalling explanation of this potential lack of competition is a regional shortage of supply in school capacity, which diminishes the schools' competition for students. In 2012 the third round of interviews and document studies revealed that though the schools had increased their capacity in the meantime, demand had gone even further up, and that the supply shortage therefore remained. Nonetheless, the schools were preparing for a decreasing number of students over the years to come, and this was reflected in an increased competitive awareness among the schools.

Nonetheless, the cooperative institutions have to a large extent remained, and overall there seems to be competing logics (Thornton & Ocasio 2008) between traditional school values focusing on general education and NPM values focusing on attracting students in competition and ensuring financial results. The interesting question could also be whether schools can succesfully compete and cooperate/collaborate at the same. Will it be possible to make some sort of public co-opetition which could introduce some competition for bettering the offers for students and at the same time insure that schools work cooperative/collaborative for the overall goals of the public, instead of just insuring their own interest?

Furthermore, there are substantial differences between the schools size and geographical placement making especially one of them vulnerable for competition – and making this school more strategically oriented. Finally, two of the schools had in 2008 participated in larger co-operative agreements and hence a merger with other schools (one with a business college the other with a more adult oriented school). Both cases are interesting because these cooperation agreements and mergers would have been unlikely before the structural reform, and we can now follow the impact of these arrangements on the strategic stance at the schools.

Though, our paper has some interesting findings we also acknowledge some important limitation. First the results may be influenced by the case selection, not so much in regard to the variation between the schools but more in regard to that they all are in the same area known for its close collaboration. The case study could potentially have shown a very in direct pattern in the very competitive highly urbanized areas. Future research would therefore benefit from studying these issues in other setting. However, a case study does not necessarily urge for generalizability like in surveys but more toward analytical generalizability (Yin 2009), and therefore we do not the specific causality. Despite these limitations, our case study has the strength of looking at the phenomenon of strategic management in concrete setting with all its complexity (Yin 2009).

REFERENCES

Adnett, N. & Davies, P. 2003. Schooling reforms in England: from quasi-markets to co-opetition? *Journal of Education Policy*, 18 (4): 393-406.

Andersen, S. C. & Serritzlew, S. 2007. The unintended effects of private school competition, *Journal of Public Administration Research and Theory*, 17 (2): 335–56.

Andrews, R., Boyne, G.A., Law, J., & Walker, R.M. 2009. Strategy formulation, strategy content and performance. *Public Management Review*, 11(1): 1-22.

Beckett, J. 2000. The "government should run like a business" mantra. *The American Review of Public Administration*, 30(2): 185-204.

Bengtsson, M., & Kock, S. 2000. " Coopetition" in business Networks—to cooperate and compete simultaneously. *Industrial Marketing Management*, 29(5): 411-426.

Boyne, G. A. 2002. Public and private management: What's the difference? *Journal of Management Studies*, 39(1): 97-122.

Boyne, G. A., & Walker, R. M. 2004. Strategy Content and Public Service Organizations, *Journal of Public Administration Research and Theory*, 14(2): 231-252.

Boyne, G. A., & Walker, R. M. 2010. Strategic management and public service performance: The way ahead. *Public Administration Review.* 70(s1): 185-s192.

Bradley, S., Crouchley, R., Millington, J., & Taylor, J. (2000). Testing for quasi-market forces in secondary education. *Oxford Bulletin of Economics and Statistics*, 62(3): 357-390.

Bryson, J. M. 2004. *Strategic planning for public and nonprofit organizations: A guide to strengthening and sustaining organizational achievement* (3rd ed.). San Francisco: Jossey-Bass.

Bryson, J.M., Berry, F.S. & Yang, K. 2010. The State of Public Strategic Management Research: A Selective Literature Review and Set of Future Directions. *The American Review of Public Administration.* 40 (5): 495-521.

Christensen, J. G. & Pallesen. T.. 2001. Institutions, Distributional Concerns and Public Sector Reform. *European Journal of Political Research,* 39: 179-202.

Christensen, T. & Lægreid, P. 2007. The Whole-of-Government Approach to Public Sector Reform. *Public Administration Review*, 67 (6): 1059-66.

Ferlie, E. 1992. The creation and evolution of quasi markets in the public sector: A problem for strategic management. *Strategic Management Journal*, 13: 79–97.

Ferlie, E. 2003. Quasi strategy: Strategic management in contemporary public sector. In A. M. Pettigrew, H. Thomas and R. Whittington (Eds.), *Handbook of Strategy and Management*: 279-298. London: Sage Publications Ltd.

Glennerster, H. 1991. Quasi-markets for education? *The Economic Journal.* 101(408): 1268-1276.

Gnyawali, D.R. He, J. & Madhavan, R. 2006. Impact of Co-Opetition on Firm Competitive Behavior: An Empirical Examination. *Journal of Management*, 32 (4): 507-530.

Gregory, R. 2003 . Theoretical Faith and Practical Works: De-Autonomizing and Joining-Up in the New Zealand State Sector. In T. Christensen & P. Lægreid (eds.), *Autonomy and Regulation: Coping with Agencies in the Modern State*: 137 – 61. Cheltenham, UK: Edward Elgar .

Hansen, J.R. 2011. Application of Strategic Management Tools after an NPM Inspired Reform: Strategy as Practice in Danish Schools. *Administration & Society*. 43(7): 770-806.

Hofer, C. W., & Schendel, D. 1978. *Strategy Formulation: Analytical Concepts*, St. Paul: West Publishing Company.

Hood, C. 1991. A public management for all seasons? *Public Administration*, 69(1): 3-19.

Hooks, J., & Palakshappa, N. 2009. Co-operation and collaboration: The case of the de-regulated new zealand electricity industry. *International Journal of Public Sector Management.* 22(4): 292-309.

Johanson, J-E. 2009. Strategy Formation in Public Agencies, *Public Administration*, 87(4): 872-891.

Jørgensen, T. B. 1999. The public sector in an in-between time: Searching for new public values. *Public Administration*, 77(3): 565-584.

Kettl, D. F. 1997. "Building Lasting Reform: Enduring Questions, Missing Answers." In Donald F. Kettl & John J. Dilulio, eds. *Inside the Reinvention Machine: Appraising Governmental Reform*. Washington, D.C.: Brookings.

Koontz, T. M., & Thomas, C. W. 2006. What do we know and need to know about the environmental outcomes of collaborative management? *Public Administration Review.* 66(s1): 111-121.

Le Grand, J. 1991. Quasi-markets and social policy. *The Economic Journal*, 101: 1256-67.

Le Grand, J. (2009). *The other invisible hand: Delivering public services through choice and competition*. Princeton: Princeton University Press.

Le Grand, J. 2010. Knights and Knaves Return: Public Service Motivation and the Delivery of Public Services. *International Public Management Journal*, 13 (1): 56-71.

Llewellyn, S., & Tappin, E. 2003. Strategy in the public sector: Management in the wilderness. *Journal of Management Studies*. 40(4): 955-982.

McGuire, M. 2006. Collaborative Public Management: Assessing What We Know and How We Know It. *Public Administration Review*, 66 (s1): 33-43.

Meier, K., O'Toole, L., Jr, Boyne, G., & Walker, R. 2007. Strategic management and the performance of public organizations: Testing venerable ideas against recent theories. *Journal of Public Administration Research and Theory*, 17(3): 357-377.

Miles, M. B. & Huberman, A. M. 1994. *Qualitative Data Analysis: An Expanded Sourcebook*. Thousand Oakes, CA: Sage Publications.

Mintzberg, H., Ahlstrand, B. W., & Lampel, J. 2009. *Strategy safari: The complete guide through the wilds of strategic management*. (2nd edition). Harlow: Financial Times Prentice Hall.

Moore, M. H. 1995. *Creating public value: Strategic management in government*. Cambridge, MA: Harvard University Press.

Moore, M. H. 2000. Managing for value: Organizational strategy in for-profit, nonprofit, and governmental organizations. *Nonprofit and Voluntary Sector Quarterly*, 29(1): 183-204.

Nutt, P. C., & Backoff, R. W. 1993. Organizational publicness and its implications for strategic management. *Journal of Public Administration Research and Theory*, 3(2): 209-231.

Olsen, J. 2006. Maybe it is time to rediscover bureaucracy. *Journal of Public Administration Research and Theory*, 16(1): 1-24.

Olson, M. 1971. *The Logic of Collective Action*. Cambridge, Ma.: Harvard University Press.

Peters, B. G., & Pierre, J. 1998. Governance without government? rethinking public administration. *Journal of Public Administration Research and Theory*. 8(2): 223-243.

Pierson, P. 2000. Increasing Returns, Path Dependence, and the Study of Politics. *The American Political Science Review*. 94 (2): 251-267.

Pollitt, C. 1990. *Managerialism and the public services: The Anglo-American experience*. Oxford: Blackwell.

Pollitt, C. 2003. *Joined-up Government: A Survey*. Political Studies Review 1: 34 – 49.

Pollitt, C., & Bouckaert, G. 2011. *Public management reform* (3rd ed.). Oxford: Oxford University Press.

Principals' Association. 2011. *Strategi 2015*. Online access April 4th 2013: www.rektorforeningen.dk/files/hovedsiderne/2011_strategi_090511.pdf

Rainey, H. G. 2009. *Understanding and Managing Public Organizations*, 4th ed. Jossey-Bass.

Ring, P. S., & Perry, J. L. 1985. Strategic management in public and private organizations: Implications of distinctive contexts and constraints. *The Academy of Management Review*, 10(2): 276-286.

Scott, W. R. 2007. *Institutions and Organizations: Ideas and Interests* (3rd ed.). Sage Publications.

Scharpf, F. W. 1994. Games Real Actors Could Play Positive and Negative Coordination in Embedded Negotiations. *Journal of Theoretical Politics*, 6 (1): 27–53.

Soss, J., Fording, R., & Schram, S. F. 2011. The organization of discipline: From performance management to perversity and punishment. *Journal of Public Administration Research and Theory*. 21(suppl 2): i203-i232.

The Danish Ministry of the Interior and Health 2004. *Agreement on a Structural Reform*. An English version of "Strukturkommissionens betænkning – sammenfatning betænkning nr. 1434". (www.im.dk/publikationer/agreement/Agreement.pdf).

Thornton, P. & Ocasio, W. 2008. Institutional Logics. In R. Greenwood C. Oliver R. Suddaby K. Sahlin-Andersson. *The SAGE Handbook of Organizational Institutionalism.* . London: SAGE Publications Ltd.

Walker, R. M., Brewer, G. A., Boyne, G. A., & Avellaneda, C. N. 2011. Market orientation and public service performance: New public management gone mad? *Public Administration Review*. 71(5): 707-717.

Walley, K. 2007. Coopetition: An introduction to the subject and an agenda for research. *International Studies of Management and Organization*, 37 (2): 11-31.

Whitty, G. 1997. Creating quasi-markets in education: A review of recent research on parental choice and school autonomy in three countries, *Review of Research in Education*, 22: 3-47.

Yin, R. 2009. *Case study research: Design and method.* (4th edition). Thousand Oaks: SAGE.

Appendix A: Coding list for interviews (used in Nvivo)

Code	Examples
The local administration	Relations, support
The regional administration, general regulation	Relations, support, funding, regulation, control
The regional administration, student related regulation	Formal and informal agreements on the distribution of students
The national administration	Regulation, laws, control, funding
Higher education	Cooperation, planning
Other schools (gymnasiums)	Contacts with other principals, agreements, disagreements
Other schools (non-gymnasiums)	Contacts with other principals, agreements, disagreements
The board	Members, chairman, internal relationships, role
Buildings	Ownership, size, quality of buildings
Students	Intake, retention, representation, quality of students
School performance	Student grades, student satisfaction, teacher satisfaction
Geographical position	Urban/rural, proximity to other schools, potential students
The business cycle	Economic pressure, birth cohorts etc.
Competition	Struggles over aspects such as students, teachers, and funding
Cooperation	Formal and informal norms about cooperation, support for other schools,
The principal	Leadership style, personal qualities, personal network etc.
Employees (teachers)	Age, areas of study, cohesion, inclusion in decision processes
Internal organization	Formal organization of school, leaders, councils

(continues)

Code	Examples
The reform	Self-government, activity-based funding
Strategy content	Strategic orientation towards various areas of interest
Strategy process	Initiation, decision, implementation, and evaluation of strategy
Strategic weaknesses	Internal aspects, which are harmful towards achieving objectives
Strategic strengths	Internal aspects, which are helpful towards achieving objectives
Course supply	Number of courses, specialization vs. generalization
Economy and finances	Budgets, accounts, funding

Appendix B: Coding categories

Strategic orientation	Coding content
External orientation	
School cooperation	Cooperative arrangements and use of networks
School competition	Competition over students, teachers, and funding
Student intake	School attention towards the number of new students enrolled
Growth	Intentions of increasing the number of students or educations
School profile	Brand, reputation, market positioning
Internal orientation	
Quality of teaching	Orientations towards the level of class room teaching
Student retention	Initiatives aimed at retaining students (for as long as possible)
Student well-being	Student satisfaction, school environment
Teacher well-being	Teacher satisfaction, work environment
Financial situation	Attention towards budgets and accounts
Efficiency (output/input)	Attention to the input-output ratio

Strategic decision-making	Coding content
Overall use of strategic management	Extent of use and formalization
Decision-making	Consensus or hierarchical (manager and board driven)
Actor roles	De-coupled,
- Principal	Role of the principal
- Board	Role of the board
- Teachers	Role of the teachers
External coordination (other secondary schools)	Coordination of strategy with other schools
Strategic tools	
- Application	Number of schools using strategic tools
- Formalization	Degree of formalization of tools used